Cut dotted lines at toes
to insert costume tabs

Edenia

Artemus

Plate 1

Glue the top and side
edges of shape to back
of hat. Slip on doll's
head

Cut a slit at hand to
insert purse or parasol

Do not cut out white
spaces between arms
and bodies

Edenia's red silk
"best" dress.

Artemus' brown
serge business
suit.

Plate 2

Glue the top and side
edges of shape to back
of hat. Slip hat on doll's
head

Do not cut out white
spaces between arms
and bodies

Cut a slit at hand to
insert parasol or hatbox

Edenia wears a
promenade dress
for a shopping
excursion.

Artemus wears
a high silk hat
and fine street
clothing.

Plate 3

Rory sails his boat. He likes to play with his rubber ball.

Annabella wears a favorite pink dress. She likes to cut out paper dolls.

On hot day, Annabella wears a lacy, white pinafore.

Cut at dotted line to insert ball

Rory is proud of his new tricycle. He wears his Sunday best to have a photograph taken.

Do not cut out white spaces between arms and bodies

Annabella is dressed up for a stroll. She carries a parasol.

Plate 4

Slightly old-fashioned dress remade from one worn by Annabella's mother.

Annabella plays outside with a doll.

Position according to arrows

Annabella says her prayers at bedtime.

Annabella's best coat.

A

To dress Annabella in the costume above, glue ends of strips to the back of costume, leaving the centers free. Slip the costume over the doll.

Annabella's "Paris" outfit was sent as a gift from her aunt.

Plate 5

Glue to back of aigrette
and perch on hair

Edenia and
Artemus attend
the opera ball.
She has remod-
eled her wedding
dress into a ball
gown.

Do not cut out white
spaces between arms
and bodies

E

Ar

Plate 6

Edenia's sister
Fauna is getting
married. Edenia
wears an orchid
silk ensemble.

Artemus, an
usher, wears a
morning suit.

E

Ar

Top hat from Plate 3
can be worn with this

Do not cut out white
spaces between arms
and bodies

Cut a slit at hand
to insert parasol

Plate 7

Rory takes his "Teddy" to sleep.

Rory wears a coat and hat exactly like his father's.

Annabella's blue velvet winter ensemble with mink trim.

Annabella, a flower girl in Aunt Fauna's wedding.

Rory, a ring bearer, wears a "Little Lord Fauntleroy" suit.

Plate 8

Glue top and side edges
of shape to back of hat.
Slip hat on doll's head

Edenia wears a
simple aquama-
rine sport dress to
play lawn croquet.

E

Artemus is com-
fortable in a linen
suit.

Ar

Do not cut out white
spaces between arms
and bodies

Plate 9

Rory, in a sailor suit, digs for seashells at the seashore.

Rory wears English tweeds to school.

Glue top and side edges of shape to the back of hat. Slip hat on doll's head

Do not cut out white spaces between arms and bodies

Rory and Annabella go to a fancy dress party. He is in Russian style; she is a rainbow.

Plate 10

Edenia delivers a
speech at a
monthly meeting
of the Ladies'
Temperance
League.

Artemus bought
this Paris gown
for his wife while
on a business trip
to New York City.

Do not cut out white
spaces between arms
and bodies

Plate 11

Cut a slit at dotted line
to insert embroidery
hoop and hatbox

Cut a slit in crook of
arm to insert parasol

Edenia attends a
garden party.

Edenia's "at
home" dress
remodeled from a
25 year old dress
which belonged to
her mother.

Plate 12

Glue the top and side edges of shape to back of hat. Slip hat on doll's head

Cut a slit to insert handkerchief

Edenia's combing jacket.

Edenia's plum velvet winter wrap, to wear over purple and black dress.

Artemus wears a coachman's coat and bowler hat.

Plate 13